I0491061

Abolish the Police

Robert J. Disario

Copyright © 2020 RobDisario.com

Cover Photography by Michael Disario

All rights reserved.

ISBN: 9798682195787

DEDICATION

To my sister, Cheryl. May Betty forever burn within-to guide and steer you in the right direction. I know deep in my heart that you will compromise and you will negotiate, but you'll never be defeated.

And if the circumstance ever presents itself, you can have one of my kidneys.

CONTENTS

DISCLAIMER

The following literary work is mine. The opinions expressed in this book do not represent my employer, my family, my cats or the imaginary dinosaur I had as a child. These opinions are of a sound mind and will not be suppressed.

1. INTRODUCTION

The police are unnecessary. In a digital age of artificial intelligence and advanced technology, the concept of an antiquated system of policing has gone the way of the taxicab. As time alters the way Americans live their lives, it's time we alter the manner in which people are held accountable. Americans use cell phones and app technology to do everything from shopping to hailing a cab. Thanks to Alexa and other voice-activated systems, we no longer need to even use a computer keyboard. We no longer have to check the air pressure in our car tires thanks to small sensors that communicate to our dashboards and determine whether we need to add air.

With technology consuming every moment of our lives, how come the criminal justice system has failed to progress in the same manner? Some argue this tech revolution is relatively new and it takes time for complex government systems like criminal justice to catch up. Frankly, this argument is weak. In truth we've been living with this technology for nearly thirty years. The tech revolution began when we used it to replace mail, data input, card catalogues in libraries, and even books themselves. Heck, the Amazon Kindle was released in November 2007, with the first working prototype, D00111, debuting in 2004. This simple but ingenious invention made Ben Franklin's library dream obsolete. As we all remember from third-grade history, it was Franklin who owned a printing press in Boston, Massachusetts. He created this idea of government-run libraries across the country. With a digital device replacing books, libraries around the country are so desperate to attract patrons that they've been reduced to hosting transgender burlesque shows for children. Many "woke" liberals assume these shows are about inclusion and acceptance, but they're really about getting people to walk through the door of an otherwise irrelevant public building. But I digress.

The purpose of this concise book is to discuss an antiquated arm of law enforcement in America. It will analyze the many facets of police work that have become obsolete. In addition, I'll discuss how society can address common behaviors or manmade issues without the need for uniformed personnel. Some points I make you will agree with, and some you won't. My only request is that you keep an open mind and continue reading. By its conclusion, I'm confident you'll understand my argument and the need for this dialogue.

In the interest of full disclosure, I must preface the following chapters by admitting I am employed as a full-time police officer. I work in an urban community that neighbors a major city in Massachusetts. I have dedicated my professional career to enforcing the law set forth by state and local governments. I may not agree with some laws I enforce, but I'm obligated by oath to take action and to hold those who commit crimes accountable.

I should also admit I'm a dinosaur in the profession. I took the job believing most people were good and only a small percentage of human filth preyed on innocent victims. I still ascribe to the idea that sheepdogs must be omnipresent to discourage wolves from bothering the flock. I have committed my time at my department to protecting people from the wolves.

My generation of cops feels sheepdogs must act swiftly and justly when wolves strike. Truth be told, I'm not convinced the newest generation of police officers have adopted this philosophy. Quite frankly, I don't care if they have. My attitude toward the job has certainly changed in the past two decades of policing, much of it to the detriment of my psyche. That's not to suggest I've become bitter or complacent; in fact, it is the opposite. I view human behavior more clearly than my wide-eyed, former rookie self.

So, without further delay, let's get to it!

2. THE CRIMINAL JUSTICE SYSTEM

The ability for a government to enforce their laws is merely one arm of the criminal justice system. The others are those who make laws and those who decide whether the law has been broken. I'm not going into a big civics lesson here because I'm assuming if you're reading this book, it is information you already have. However, there is an important point I need to illuminate. Those who make the law, albeit federal government, state legislature or local body, never consider how newly created laws will be enforced. Several communities in eastern Massachusetts, for example, have enacted laws restricting the use of handheld leaf blowers to certain times of the year (spring and fall). So, you may ask, who enforces that? Fish and game wardens? Public works? Park police? Nope. In these communities, the local police department is given the unwelcome task of enforcement. Seems odd local governments are turning the screws on their residents by sending uniformed police officers for a seemingly trivial crime. It's ironic, especially in an anti-police culture where police are trying to forge relationships with their constituents, to have the town's top brass sending officers to cite for a relatively minor infraction.

The other arm of the criminal justice system is those who determine whether the law was broken. This includes lawyers, judges and elected district attorneys. How is this branch of the system doing? Well, Suffolk County District Attorney Rachel Rollins stated publicly that her office will no longer prosecute low-level crimes like trespassing, shoplifting or assault and battery on a police officer. I'd argue this arm is not functioning either.

Seems as though every branch of the criminal justice system has its unique set of problems. Unfortunately, the common thread in today's society is to focus angry energy on updating police services. The easy answer is to accuse police departments from coast to coast of employing racist, bigoted cops. Many who make this claim have hard evidence of people of color, specifically young black men, being terrorized mostly by white officers. Oftentimes, video evidence of this bullying is broadcasted via social media and cable news, branding the footage as "viral." Many of these videos are disturbing to say the least. Let's take for example the police-worn body camera video shooting of black seventeen-year-old Laquan McDonald in Chicago. Unfortunately, when this video went viral, there was no context to explain what led up to this shooting. As a result, Chicago Police Officer Jason Van Dyke was convicted of murder and sentenced to six years in prison. Whether or not you agree with the outcome, this case was smoking-gun evidence that black men were being killed by white police officers.

If what I lay out in the following pages were adopted by the City of Chicago before this incident, many would argue Laquan McDonald would still be alive. I'm not so sure. It seems Laquan McDonald had several problems, the least of which involved the Chicago Police. But that's a discussion for another book. What I'd like to stress is the fact that dangerous encounters, like that of Van Dyke and MacDonald, could be prevented with the absolution of the police. I begin my argument with a history of the police profession. In the next chapter, I'll offer a brief lesson on the major operational components of policing in the twentieth century, and you'll decide for yourself if it's time for a change.

3. ANTIQUATED POLICING

America is still policing as we were a hundred years ago. Early twentieth-century police officers were tasked with patrolling the settlements on foot, providing security and responding to criminal activity. Larger cities and towns had blue call boxes mounted on street corners throughout the town that were hardwired to the dispatch center. Those boxes would have little telephones inside and would ring the dispatch center. The officer would use a call box key to open the front lid and ring dispatch. The dispatcher would advise him of any service calls and the officer would respond appropriately. Obviously, there would be a significant delay in officer response due to the officer calling only periodically. By the time the officer got the information from dispatch and responded to the area, the suspects were often either gone or the issue had resolved itself.

Enter the age of the police radio. According to Engineering and Technology History Wiki (ethw.org), Detroit Police Officers Kenneth Cox and Robert L. Batts installed the first radio in their Model T police car in 1928. The dispatcher would alert patrol officers of crimes in progress, such as stolen cars and descriptions of missing children. A plaque commemorating this momentous ingenuity is at the harbormaster station on Belle Island of Detroit, Michigan. Eventually, every police department in America implemented this innovation to provide better police service to their communities. The 1960s and 70s introduced the portable "walkie-talkie" style radio that police use to this day. The technology has improved over time to include smaller batteries, lighter equipment and digital voice as opposed to analog. Even though portable radios have come a long way in 91 years, we're still using this outdated technology.

In addition to outdated communication, the way police enforce the law is antiquated. For much of the twentieth century, police officers proactively patrolled to deter, to prevent and to stop crimes in progress. This was accomplished by an approach called proactive policing, which was a large part of law enforcement during the latter half of the century. Many would argue the landmark decision Terry v. Ohio set the standard for this approach to law enforcement. The theory argued that a police officer could base his decision to investigate on a hunch. The cop in the Terry v. Ohio case had a hunch that Terry was up to no good, so officer surveilled Terry for several minutes. Terry was acting "squirrely" (an industry term), so the cop made a threshold inquiry and pat-frisked him for weapons.

Until this U.S. Supreme Court decision, the fourth amendment specifically prevented police officers from searching anybody without probable cause...no matter what. The Terry v. Ohio Supreme Court decision decided the fourth amendment did not apply to Terry because the officer had reasonable suspicion to believe Terry was armed. And he was right. As a result of good police work, the cop discovered Terry was in possession of an illegal firearm and planning to rob a store. How did this officer establish reasonable suspicion? The answer is simple: by simply watching his behavior.

This would be an unacceptable practice in 2020.

The law enforcement community recognizes there has been a sudden shift in American policing. Just as the 60s and 70s brought the paradigm shift where police began to rely on public trust, the job of crime enforcement is changing. The law enforcement community had progressed significantly in the 90s and 00s, where the police and the public were partners working hard to maintain safety. It wasn't that long ago when a uniformed police officer could approach anybody on the street for a brief chat. As of four or five years ago, most citizens welcomed the interactions. This cooperation between the public and the police set an unwritten contract in motion. We agreed that once certain information was obtained by the officer, each would go on about their day. If, however, the officer gained information that raised his suspicions, there were procedural laws the officer followed to arrest, summons or take no criminal action. This cooperation was thanks to a community police effort in the 90s when local governments began to realize they were ineffective without help. They instituted community policing (CP) policies that made street cops appear less threatening and more approachable. The CP theory hypothesizes that if the cops seemed friendlier, the locals would trust them with important information about the happenings in the neighborhood. It also helped display local cops in normal, non-threatening situations. Sounds like a no-brainer. It was a successful, common-sense approach until the money ran out.

When the economy began to suffer in the early 2000s, local municipalities no longer had the funds to continue community policing programs. Despite dwindling funds, police departments attempted to incorporate CP programs piecemeal. However, actual police work got in the way. For example, when CP officers were taken out of their "lolli-cop" positions and put back into sector cars, they didn't have time to visit the neighborhood bar-b-que because the local convenience store had been robbed.

Enter 2014, where the police have become a uniformed representation of an oppressive American government. Where celebrities and athletes wear pig socks and take a knee during the national anthem to voice their opposition. Where everyone has a video camera in their pocket, and they begin recording cops doing their job to emphasize the subtext of racism. Some force a narrative where everybody believes black lives no longer matter, and they start an organization that precipitates this misnomer. Local police officer Darren Wilson is then vilified for what was described as a brutal killing of a young black teen. All that sounded like a good idea in 2014.

A 2018 viral cell phone video in Boston, MA, illustrates why cops shouldn't speak with anyone without a smoking gun in their hand while they are standing over a cooling corpse. The video depicts two plain clothes officers sitting in their parked, unmarked cruiser. A guy approaches and initiates a conversation while filming with his cell phone camera. Understandably, the cop reacts by asking the citizen why he's filming, which seems like a reasonable reaction. The cop never swears at the citizen, or touches him, and the citizen is allowed to leave without recourse.

As a result of this interaction, the anti-cop climate activates into hyperdrive. They label the cops as racist and demand their termination. The citizen sues the Boston Police Department—for what, I think we'll never know. As a knee-jerk reaction, the department decides to put every officer through so-called sensitivity training, as if they had done something wrong. Viral videos like this one have alienated the local officer. She is now discouraged from merely speaking to another citizen. She can no longer interact with another human without being chastised by his superiors, which include the mayor of the city (as in the Boston case). The new cop attitude is a reversal of the officer in the Terry v. Ohio case. I fear a police officer today may see a crime and fail to act for fear the interaction will be posted on YouTube.

This is our new reality in American policing.

I contend we are again facing a paradigm shift. This is due to several factors, including technology and a disillusioned accountability for individual officers. I explain this in much more detail in my book *#Nationwide Police Strike*. But more alarming and concerning for the general public is the failure of the profession to attract qualified candidates. As a result of the anti-police era, people are viewing the police profession less favorably than they once did. Today, police officers are disrespected for no reason other than wearing a uniform. A good example of this was the summer of 2019 when citizens dumped buckets of water on cops. Most don't aspire to be treated like a lesser human.

So, rather than forcing officers into impossible situations of viral cell phone videos and lack of support from the community, why hasn't American policing adopted innovative, cutting-edge approaches to policing? With the modern manner in which we read books, purchase household items on Amazon and apply for a job, why can't law enforcement catch up? These approaches would solve the problem of police-related violence as well as the recruiting issue.

We begin our analysis with a tutorial of what police do. In the next chapter, we'll walk through four hours of a typical day for a specific police department in Massachusetts. We'll define specifically what they do and review how their time is spent. Is this antiquated system of policing worth our tax dollars? Let's find out.

4. WHAT POLICE OFFICERS DO

In preparation for this book, I analyzed the call log of a large city police department to determine what cops do on a regular basis. Brockton, Massachusetts, is a diverse, urban community just south of Boston. According to their website, Brockton is a city of just more than ninety-five thousand residents. The city was originally a manufacturing town that settled in 1700 and became incorporated in 1881. Nicknamed "Shoe City," Brockton quickly became known for their textiles, similar to many New England communities at the turn of the twentieth century. Brockton's demographics in 2019 were 42% white, 43% African American, and 7% Hispanic/Latino. It encompasses 21 square miles of land and has a median income of $34,255. Needless to say, it's a large, diverse community steeped in American history. The Brockton Police Department consists of just over two hundred sworn police officers sharing the load in three different shifts.

In my review, I found the daily call log for the Brockton Police Department on their website. If you're a novice to police duties, I encourage you to visit their website (http://www.brocktonpolice.com/category/police-log/) and look at a random day. For the purpose of this book, I randomly retrieved the call log from an average weekday so readers could get a glimpse of police work. The following is the actual call log beginning at approximately 7am in the morning on August 15, 2019. After each entry, I offer a brief description of each call as I interpret it. I copied and pasted it directly from the department's website, so nothing has been omitted. I should note, I chose Brockton Massachusetts Police Department because it has a larger-than-average city population and is busier than the vast majority of police departments in Massachusetts. Due to its size and call volume, the department employs more officers than most departments in the state. I did not want to give the impression that I purposely chose a department that is not busy or has a lot of crime. Just the opposite. I chose Brockton because the department has a large call volume. In addition, my intent in analyzing this particular police department is not to disparage or impugn their officers or organization, but simply to illustrate the common duties of the average police department. And I can't stress this enough: I have no affiliation with the City of Brockton or with their police department. (Note: the last name of officer and dispatcher/call taker has been omitted.)

Brockton Police Call Log August 15, 2019

19-89700 0655 Check Motorist Drive Erratic Unfounded / Nothing Located

Call Taker: Telephone Operator Edmar

Location/Address: TORREY ST

ID: Patrolman Brian

Disp-06:59:21 Arvd-07:12:20 Clrd-07:20:15

This call was received at 6:55 am. The caller complained about a motorist who was operating recklessly on Torrey Street. Citizens became frustrated in traffic and called the emergency line to report another commuter driving recklessly. According to the call back, the patrol officer checked the area but was unable to locate the offending vehicle. This outcome is not uncommon. Unfortunately, what most complainants don't know is even if the responding officer located the vehicle, there is no enforcement action taken.

19-89701 0703 911 Verify Call False 911 Call

Call Taker: Telephone Operator Melanie

Location/Address: 83 AUBURN ST

ID: Patrolman Robert

Disp-07:28:13 Enrt-07:30:19 Arvd-07:39:34 Clrd-08:02:32

This call was for someone who accidentally dialed the emergency line, 911. The dispatched officer was responsible for responding to the location and confirming that the call was actually accidental. There may be times when officers discover the call was not accidental and in fact there is an emergency. Although a possibility, it happens very infrequently.

19-89702 0711 911 Verify Call FALSE ALARM

Call Taker: Telephone Operator Edmar

Location/Address: [BRO 316] 835 OAK ST

ID: Patrolman Hermer

Disp-07:17:03 Arvd-07:22:34 Clrd-07:26:05

Similar to the false 911 call, this was for someone who accidentally activated a commercial burglar alarm. This is a common occurrence during the morning hours. Employees arriving for work commonly input the wrong passcode or enter an area of the building they did not know was alarmed. This particular location was a branch of a local bank. The officer responding to the location was tasked with checking the building to assure it was not being burglarized or to confirm that the activation was accidental. A thorough officer will identify any persons on scene and ensure they're actually an employee.

19-89703 0711 911 Unknown Emergency Unfounded / Nothing Located

Call Taker: Telephone Operator Melanie

Location/Address: 66 MELROSE AVE

ID: Patrolman Mark

Disp-07:16:28 Enrt-07:18:28 Arvd-07:20:57 Clrd-07:53:16

An "unknown emergency" is most likely a caller who made contact with the dispatcher without explaining what their emergency was. The officer is responsible for responding to the location and addressing the nature of the emergency. In most instances, the call was misdialed, and no emergency existed.

19-89705 0719 911 Transfer to Ambulance Taken/Referred to Other Agency

Call Taker: Telephone Operator Edmar

I'm not exactly sure of the nature of this call other than the dispatcher sent it directly to the private ambulance company that services the city. As you can see, no police officer was assigned or dispatched to any particular location.

19-89706 0722 Check Property Matter Settled

Call Taker: School Police Officer Michael

Location/Address: [BRO 35] 105 KEITH AVE

ID: School Police Officer Michael

Arvd-07:24:09 Clrd-07:29:10

This particular location is one of Brockton's elementary schools. The school police officer appears to have been checking the physical security of the school for five minutes. As you'll see in the next several entries in the log, the officer made his rounds, ensuring the buildings were secure. I assume these checks do not happen during the school year.

19-89709 0729 Check Property Matter Settled

Call Taker: School Police Officer Michael

Location/Address: [BRO 1948] 1121 WARREN AVE

ID: School Police Officer Michael

Arvd-07:30:45 Clrd-07:33:25

19-89710 0739 Check Property Matter Settled

Call Taker: School Police Officer Michael

Location/Address: [BRO 1534] 135 BELMONT ST

ID: School Police Officer Michael

Arvd-07:40:51 Clrd-07:44:41

19-89713 0746 911 Transfer to Ambulance
Taken/Referred to Other Agency

Call Taker: Telephone Operator Edmar

This call is the same "transfer call" as above.

19-89716 0746 SUSPICIOUS MV Clear No Action Needed

Brockton Police Department Press Log Page: 4

Dispatch Log From: 08/15/2019 Thru: 08/16/2019 0000 - 0000 Printed: 08/16/2019

Call Taker: Telephone Operator Edmar

Location/Address: 517 CENTRE ST

ID: Patrolman Joe

Disp-08:16:44 Enrt-08:18:19 Arvd-08:18:32 Clrd-08:32:48

Suspicious motor vehicles and suspicious people are very common. Basically, a resident observes someone acting "suspiciously" and calls the police to have them checked out. What the public does not know is the police are somewhat restricted when responding to these calls. Unless the reporting person can stipulate what crime was being committed, police intervention is unlikely. A person in his car eating a sandwich has every right to be there. Police officers responding to this call would be wise to take a moment to confirm whether their activity is actually suspicious before interacting with them. It's likely this call is a matter of the resident just not liking that particular person in their neighborhood. If the officer fails to approach the situation with care, their encounter may lead to a confrontation caught on camera. In this particular case, it appears the officer responded, assessed the activity and cleared the call with no police action.

Three more checks on a public school by the resource officer:

19-89715 0750 Check Property Matter Settled

Call Taker: School Police Officer Michael

Location/Address: [BRO 2259] 271 WEST ST

ID: School Police Officer Michael

Arvd-07:51:43 Clrd-07:57:24

19-89718 0804 Check Property Matter Settled

Call Taker: School Police Officer Michael

Location/Address: [BRO 3967] 45 OAKDALE ST

ID: School Police Officer Michael

Arvd-08:05:24 Clrd-08:07:33

19-89719 0811 Check Property Matter Settled

Call Taker: School Police Officer Michael

Location/Address: [BRO 2779] 180 COLONEL BELL DR

ID: School Police Officer Michael

Arvd-08:12:25 Clrd-08:24:35

19-89720 0812 911 Transfer to Ambulance
Taken/Referred to Other Agency

Call Taker: Telephone Operator Darrelyn

Another transfer to the private ambulance company. No police involvement.

19-89725 0838 Check Property Matter Settled

Call Taker: School Police Officer Michael

Location/Address: [BRO 36] 108 OAK ST

ID: School Police Officer Michael

Arvd-08:39:54 Clrd-08:46:03

19-89726 0839 B & E MV Investigation Report taken

Call Taker: Telephone Operators Nicole

Location/Address: 39 NORMAN RD

ID: Patrolman Joe

Disp-09:01:37 Enrt-09:07:20 Arvd-09:18:07 Clrd-
10:12:32

Finally, a crime! We've reviewed two hours of the police
call log and we finally have our first crime.
Unfortunately, this crime appears to have been
committed during the previous night. By the time the
victim finds his violated car, the criminal is long gone.
One item of note is this call was received by the
dispatcher at 8:39am and the officer arrived on scene at
9:17am (a duration of thirty-eight minutes). Believe it or
not, this is not an uncommon delay in police work.
Many factors determine a delay in police response,
including workload, the physical location of the
responding officer, or even vehicular traffic. As one

would imagine, officers answering calls during the overnight hours respond quicker than those who work during the day. Consider this: in the amount of time it took for this officer to respond to Norman Rd (38 minutes), the victim could have self-reported this crime though a web-based reporting portal (if one existed). I will discuss alternatives to police response in a later chapter.

19-89734 0855 Check Property Matter Settled

Call Taker: School Police Officer Michael

Location/Address: [BRO 2422] 125 OAK ST

ID: School Police Officer Michael

Arvd-08:57:19 Clrd-08:57:40

Same as above.

19-89738 0901 911 Transfer to Ambulance Taken/Referred to Other Agency

Call Taker: Telephone Operator Darrelyn

Same as above.

19-89739 0904 Check Property Matter Settled

Call Taker: School Police Officer Michael

Location/Address: [BRO 374] 472 N MAIN ST

ID: School Police Officer Michael

Arvd-09:05:56 Clrd-09:14:33

Same as above.

19-89743 0907 Hit & Run Investigate Report taken

Call Taker: Telephone Operator Nicole

Location/Address: [BRO 993] 701 BELMONT ST

ID: Patrolman Patrick

Disp-09:13:59 Enrt-09:14:55 Arvd-09:19:37 Clrd-
10:05:32

ID: Patrolman Steven

Disp-09:40:19 Arvd-09:40:26 Clrd-09:42:57

Patrolman Peter

ID: Patrolman Jonathan

Disp-09:41:29 Arvd-09:41:34 Clrd-09:54:41

ID: Patrolman Patrick

Disp-10:18:52 Arvd-10:19:04 Clrd-11:00:42

At 9:07 am, it appears the dispatcher received a call for a traffic accident where one of the vehicles fled after the crash. At first glance, this service call appears serious. It's not uncommon in cases of "leaving the scene of a motor vehicle accident" that one officer is dispatched to make contact with the victim while other officers are tasked with searching for the fleeing car. Without additional information concerning the fleeing vehicle, the case will never be investigated, and the fleeing vehicle will not be located. Thus, the victim's insurance company is the only victim. The company is forced to make repairs without holding the other operator accountable. This is the primary reason every motor vehicle is required to have insurance.

19-89740 0908 Animal Complaint Matter Settled

Call Taker: Telephone Operator Robert

Location/Address: 0 RICHMOND ST @ 52 BATTLES ST

ID: Animal Control Brian

Disp-09:11:44 Enrt-09:11:53 Arvd-09:16:35 Clrd-09:18:55

One of my favorite police service calls: the elusive animal complaint. In some communities, the animal control officer (ACO) is a civilian employee who reports to the town's health department. In others, the police department is responsible for employing an ACO who are sworn, academy-trained police officers. Smaller communities leave animal complaint calls to the average, on-duty patrol officer. In either event, animal control officers (ACO) are tasked with responding to animal calls and mitigating the complaint. In this case, it appears the ACO Brian settled whatever the matter was.

19-89741 0910 911 Transfer to Ambulance Taken/Referred to Other Agency

Call Taker: Telephone Operator Darrelyn

Same as above.

19-89747 0917 911 Transfer to Ambulance Taken/Referred to Other Agency

Call Taker: Telephone Operator Nicole

Same as above.

19-89748 0923 Check Property Matter Settled

Call Taker: School Police Officer Michael

Location/Address: [BRO 6772] 175 WARREN AVE

ID: School Police Officer Michael

Arvd-09:25:29 Clrd-09:35:20

Same as above.

19-89750 0928 MOTOR VEHICLE STOP Citation/Warning Issued

Call Taker: Sergeant William

Location/Address: 348 CRESCENT ST

ID: Sergeant William

Arvd-09:30:39 Clrd-09:39:24

One of the primary duties of the average patrol officer is traffic enforcement. This particular traffic stop was conducted by an officer with the rank of sergeant who issued the operator a warning. Every municipality is issued state-specific citation books to document the operator, the time, day and observed violations. Most of the time, this happens without incident. However, in recent years, with the universal adoption of the anti-police mentality, interactions during traffic enforcement have become contentious confrontations. In a later chapter, I'll explain how technology has made traffic stops obsolete.

19-89751 0933 Assist Fire or Ambulance Cancelled

Call Taker: Telephone Operator Robert

Location/Address: [BRO 8048] 37 EXCHANGE ST

ID: Patrolman Isaiah

Disp-09:35:20 Clrd-09:39:22

This call appears to have been to assist the Brockton Fire Department with a "fire run." Fire fighters are routinely activated for fire alarms, water leaks, motor vehicle accidents, carbon monoxide detector activations as well as a host of other emergency needs. The primary purpose of a police officer on fire calls is to assist with vehicular traffic. Fire trucks are big and clumsy. Depending on the location of the emergency, these road whales can obstruct lanes, streets and commuters. Thus, the function of police is to get the traffic around the obstructions.

19-89753 0938 911 Hang Up False 911 Call

Call Taker: Telephone Operator Darrelyn

Location/Address: 1027 WARREN AVE Apt. #1

ID: Patrolman Isaiah

Disp-09:42:41 Arvd-09:44:54 Clrd-09:53:13

Another 9-1-1 hang-up call.

19-89756 0951 Check Property Matter Settled

Call Taker: School Police Officer Michael

Location/Address: [BRO 2437] 125 PEARL ST

ID: School Police Officer Michael

Arvd-09:52:44 Clrd-10:02:55

Same as above.

19-89759 0954 Unwanted Guest Drunk Matter Settled

Call Taker: Telephone Operator Darrelyn

Location/Address: [BRO 1448] 304 MAIN ST

ID: Patrolman Steven

Disp-09:57:15 Arvd-10:04:39 Clrd-10:05:32

Patrolman Peter

ID: Patrolman Robert

Arvd-10:03:21 Clrd-10:05:06

304 Main Street is the public library in Brockton. I'm not exactly sure why a library patron was drunk at ten o'clock in the morning, but it appears the police responded and assisted him out of the building. Without knowing more about this call, my suspicion is the "unwanted guest" was a homeless individual on the property whom library staff wanted removed.

19-89758 0955 MOTOR VEHICLE STOP No Citation Issued

Call Taker: Patrolman Isaiah

Location/Address: 10 FOREST AVE

ID: Patrolman Isaiah

Arvd-09:54:53 Clrd-10:03:05

Another traffic stop that may have been accomplished by the use of technology (more on that later).

19-89761 0957 Check Property Clear No Action Needed

Call Taker: School Police Officer Jonathan

Location/Address: [BRO 34] 464 CENTRE ST

ID: School Police Officer Jonathan

Arvd-10:00:58 Clrd-10:15:27

Same as above.

19-89762 0958 911 Transfer Out of Town
Taken/Referred to Other Agency

Call Taker: Telephone Operator Nicole

Location: [ATT]

Same as above.

19-89763 0959 911 Hang Up Unfounded / Nothing
Located

Call Taker: Telephone Operator Darrelyn

Location/Address: 23 DENTON ST Apt. #2

ID: Patrolman Joshua

Disp-10:02:39 Enrt-10:02:46 Arvd-10:10:31 Clrd-
10:17:23

Another 9-1-1 hang-up call where the officer responded
and found no emergency services required.

19-89768 1007 911 Transfer to Ambulance
Taken/Referred to Other Agency

Call Taker: Telephone Operator Nicole

Same as above.

19-89772 1014 Alarm Telephone FALSE ALARM

Call Taker: Telephone Operator Darrelyn

Location/Address: [BRO 11118] 198 TRIBOU ST

ID: Patrolman Joshua

Disp-10:17:45 Enrt-10:18:47 Arvd-10:22:43 Clrd-10:25:25

Another call for someone who accidentally activated a commercial burglar alarm.

19-89775 1017 Overdose Transported to Hospital

Call Taker: Telephone Operator Darrelyn

Location/Address: [BRO 863] 180 CENTRE ST

ID: Patrolman Robert

Disp-10:20:50 Arvd-10:21:48 Clrd-10:38:43

Don't do drugs. This was a service call where a person was transported to the hospital after overdosing on a controlled substance (drugs). As outlined in an earlier call, a major facet of the police response is traffic control around emergency apparatuses. Ambulances also fall into this category. However, for this particular call, police officers were dispatched to render emergency first aid and CPR. A police officer's training also includes the use of an AED and the facilitation of Narcan. Narcan is a stimulant that opens the receptors and reverses the effects of an opiate high. The deployment of Narcan has saved many drug-fueled lives in recent years. Since patrol officers are on the road 24/7, they are able to respond quickly and deploy life-saving measures. However, once highly trained paramedics arrive on the scene, the cops will pull back and return to their traffic duties.

In a later chapter, we'll discuss whether police officers responding to drug-related calls is actually necessary. Oftentimes, people involved in drugs are reluctant to call 911 for fear of police developing a criminal case for drug crimes. Thus, needed medical aid is delayed until it becomes too late. Whether their concerns are imagined or not, wouldn't it be ideal to have a process where law enforcement response was not necessary? More about that in chapter 6.

19-89776 1019 911 Transfer to Ambulance
Taken/Referred to Other Agency

Call Taker: Telephone Operator Darrelyn

Same as above.

19-89777 1021 MOTOR VEHICLE STOP Citation/Warning
Issued

Call Taker: Patrolman Antonio

Location/Address: 385 N QUINCY ST

ID: Patrolman Antonio

Arvd-10:21:20 Clrd-10:42:23

Same as above.

19-89778 1023 911 Transfer Out of Town
Taken/Referred to Other Agency

Call Taker: Telephone Operator Robert

19-89779 1023 911 Transfer Out of Town
Taken/Referred to Other Agency

Call Taker: Telephone Operator Nicole

19-89781 1025 911 Transfer to Ambulance
Taken/Referred to Other Agency

Call Taker: Telephone Operator Robert

19-89782 1032 MOTOR VEHICLE STOP Citation/Warning
Issued

Call Taker: School Police Officer Jonathan

Location/Address: [BRO 2089] 706 MONTELLO ST

ID: School Police Officer Jonathan

Arvd-10:34:43 Clrd-10:47:41

Same as above.

19-89783 1034 M V A - No PI Report taken

Call Taker: Telephone Operator Nicole

Location/Address: 283 N CARY ST

ID: Patrolman Joe

Disp-10:36:03 Enrt-10:36:42 Arvd-10:46:45 Clrd-12:30:34

This was a motor vehicle accident between two cars; no injuries were reported. What's noteworthy with this call is most states have laws that dictate a motorist obligation when involved in a car accident. These include exchanging information with the other operator without the aid of a police officer. Unfortunately, modern-day motorists can't seem to function without on-the-scene instructions. I contend as long as motorists follow the laws, police response is unnecessary.

19-89784 1035 DISTURBANCE Matter Settled

Call Taker: Telephone Operator Robert

Location/Address: 96 MAIN ST @ 1 CHURCH ST

ID: Patrolman Steven

Disp-10:38:02 Enrt-10:38:11 Arvd-10:47:57 Clrd-11:08:16

Patrolman Peter

A so-called disturbance is anything the caller deems it to be. This can range from a coffee patron assaulting a barista to a flock of birds landing on a playground structure (yes, an actual emergency service call). Unfortunately, in this particular case, we do not know what the disturbance was other than it was resolved.

19-89786 1041 Community Police Call Clear No Action Needed

Call Taker: Patrolman Richard

Location/Address: [BRO 1910] 53 PLYMOUTH ST

ID: Patrolman Richard

Arvd-10:42:15 Clrd-13:09:41

19-89787 1044 MOTOR VEHICLE STOP Citation/Warning Issued

Call Taker: Patrolman Antonio

Location/Address: 422 N QUINCY ST

ID: Patrolman Antonio

Arvd-10:44:50 Clrd-10:54:05

19-89791 1058 MOTOR VEHICLE STOP Citation/Warning Issued

Call Taker: Patrolman Antonio

Location/Address: [BRO 4318] 762 COURT ST

ID: Patrolman Antonio

Arvd-10:58:42 Clrd-11:04:4

Same as above.

The preceding list consisted of a four-hour call log from a typical American police department. The purpose was to illustrate the needlessness of police activity. Some of my critics may assume I browsed several call logs in search of the dullest day I could find. Nothing could be further from the truth. I chose the day prior to the start of this project (August 15, 2019). I visited the Brockton Police Department website and copied four hours of the previous day. I deleted nothing other than the last names of the dispatchers and police officers. If you're still unconvinced, please visit their website and download the call log for yourself. If the average

American took time to read this chapter and the typical day in the life of a police officer, I'm confident they'd support my argument in abolishing the police.

In the following chapter, I'll attempt to explain why the police have become an unnecessary burden on society. In addition, I'll introduce programs the criminal justice system can implement so society can function without police. Is it possible to enforce the law without uniformed police officers? Many of the following systems have already been adopted in other government applications and need nothing more than to be adapted to modern policing. Without further ado, let's explore them.

5. IN LIEU OF

After reading the call log in the previous chapter, you may say to yourself, "Geez, that seemed to be a rather busy four hours for the Brockton Police Department." On many levels, you may be right. My question is, what was actually accomplished? Of all the busy work, how many crimes were addressed, solved or prevented? Let's break down several categories of calls and discuss what could have been done in lieu of a police officer response.

Building Checks

We note in our call log, School Police Officer Michael conducted several checks of public buildings. I argue these are unnecessary. By merely reviewing the call log, I'm not clear as to what this assignment actually entails. However, I'm confident it could be replaced by several surveillance cameras placed strategically in and around the building. If the purpose of this assignment was to check the condition of the building, i.e., whether or not a window was broken or unsecured for any reason, I'm sure a surveillance camera could do the same at half the cost. Any damage not witnessed by cameras would eventually be discovered in due time. There are surveillance cameras on the market with motion-activated alerts to raise the attention of a dispatcher, or a private third party to alert the necessary personnel. For example, if youths smashed a window of the building, the person tasked with monitoring the cameras could alert a glass company (or other construction entity) to respond and replace the glass. Pretty simple. If the surveillance cameras alerted that youths were "tagging" the side of the building, the monitor could alert a graffiti removal company. Thus, the purpose of an officer checking these buildings at 9 am in the morning is wasteful and unnecessary.

Traffic Enforcement

On several occasions, the call log noted officers conducting traffic stops of morning commuters. Traffic enforcement and traffic safety is a primary function of the modern-day police officer. However, is it necessary? Do we need an army of uniformed police officers tasked with inconveniencing morning commuters with relatively minor violations? Technological advancements can be deployed to maintain traffic safety. This technology would be more reliable and consistent in enforcement. For example, so-called "red light cameras" have been in use in America since the early 90s. The function of these cameras is to film the intersection at the time the traffic signal turns red. If a vehicle goes through the intersection after the light turned red, the camera takes a picture of the license plate. Administrative personnel are responsible for reviewing the photos and mailing the operator a citation. What's more, surveillance cameras offer no bias and make no decisions based on race, color, religion or any other identifying entity. Ingenious! By using modern technology, a human police officer would no longer be tasked with waiting to observe a violation, chasing the violators and issuing a citation. This avoids the risk to the public if the suspect fails to stop, which forces the officer to chase down the violator. In addition, the camera system protects the officer from harm while conducting a traffic stop.

Another deployable technological advance is global positioning unit or GPS. This technology is now installed on almost every car sold in America today. GPS technology knows where the vehicle is at any given time, identifying the street as well the traffic regulations. Several insurance companies have implemented safe driving programs where the driver is issued a device to plug into the computer of their car.

The device monitors driving habits, and she receives insurance rate discounts for good driving. My assumption is that the device is monitoring the driver's location, speed, hard braking, evasive steering and the like. How else would they credit their customers with a discount? Nevertheless, I'm convinced GPS technology has the capacity to know the speed limit on any given street and to monitor how fast your vehicle is travelling. What if, instead of a highway patrol officer sitting by the side of the road, the car's GPS system alerted law enforcement when the vehicle was speeding? Or better yet, when a new driver is issued a license, what if the state issue's one of these devices to monitor their driving and mails them citations if it detects a violation? In essence, just as red light cameras, this technology would alert an administrator and mail the operator a citation, eliminating the need for police traffic enforcement.

Many contrarians would argue privacy concerns when GPS technology is deployed by the government. Having big brother watching your every move is unsettling. I'd argue that if this was really a concern, doubters would delete their social media accounts and throw away their cell phones. These two entities are tracking your every move, and unless you're willing to abstain, your argument about big brother is moot.

Another daily traffic-related issue flooding dispatcher phone lines is parking complaints. In more populated areas, frustrated citizens call the police to report parking violations that affect and annoy them. A common example is a parked vehicle blocking a driveway. The officer responds, makes her observation and acts accordingly. Most times, this amounts to writing a parking ticket or calling a tow truck. But that begs the question, why is a police officer tasked with such a marginal task? Most communities that suffer these types of violations employ sworn civilians to fan out across the city and write parking tickets. They're affectionately referred to as "meter-maids." There's even been cable television shows following these "warriors of the pen," who document interactions they have with violators (it's unbelievable the amount of abuse they take).

In our new, policeless system, dispatch centers can farm parking complaint calls to meter-maids. Meter-maids are paid less than police officers, require less training and avoid confrontation. Those calls that require a tow truck can be sorted accordingly, eliminating the need for a police response.

Arrests

The purpose of placing a suspect under arrest is to

identify them and bring them before a judge. Contrary to popular belief, an arrest by a police officer is not a punishment. In early twentieth century, American law enforcement agencies had limited technological resources. What little data they did have was stored in filing cabinets at the police station. Thus, to identify suspected crime-doers, officers were forced to take them into custody and attempt to identify them. This included fingerprints, criminal files with photos, etc. Previous to the middle of the century, police officers used ink and paper to gather fingerprints, and they were saved on index cards in the department's file cabinets. This archaic system had many faults. One of which is if a suspect was arrested in another community, the police would never know. A criminal could go town to town, state to state without anybody getting wise to his criminal history. It was for this reason many federal law enforcement agencies were introduced. The U.S. Marshal's Office, for example, was tasked with travelling the country executing warrants issued by district and circuit courts. Law enforcement has come a long way since, but evidently not far enough.

For those who don't know, let me explain today's arrest procedures. Once a suspect is deemed under arrest, he is secured with handcuffs and brought to the police station in a transport vehicle. At the station, he is processed by the booking officer; this process includes obtaining his fingerprints and photograph (this consists of a mug-shot and photographs of scars, marks and tattoos). The purpose of photographs is obviously to identify the subject today as well as in the future. Fingerprints are captured and stored in the event the suspect gives a fake name in a future arrest.

All fingerprints captured by American law enforcement agencies are submitted through the automated fingerprint identification system (AFIS). The prints are digitally evaluated and searched through the database for matches. Thus, if the arrestee has been arrested anywhere in America, his information will be returned to the arresting agency within hours.

In the age of wireless devices, fingerprint technology, mobile computers and high-tech photography, if the purpose of arrest is truly for identification, why can't the police gather the information they need on the scene and send the suspect on his way? Is there mobile technology available that allows street officers to capture the identification markers without seizing the suspect and bringing him to the police station? Let's remember: the onsite arrest by a police officer is not to be used as punishment. This bears repeating: arrest by police after an alleged crime is not punitive. The purpose of arrest is to identify the subject. The necessary equipment to accomplish a booking procedure is already deployed by most police departments, thus eliminating the need for arrest. For example, digital cameras are as accessible as cell phones, and fingerprint technology is evolving every day. A company called Integrated Biometrics promises ten fingerprints in ten seconds with their Kojak fingerprint scanner. This machine and many like it are already being used in the United Kingdom. According to a February 2018 article in *WiredUK*, "The system being used by West Yorkshire Police searches the 12 million fingerprint records kept in the UK's criminal and immigration databases" (wired.co.uk).

Why are United Kingdom police services lightyears ahead of American law enforcement? This technology and more like it could greatly reduce the number of violent police encounters by encouraging suspects and citizens alike to cooperate with the law. Many argue the risk of going to jail (even for a short period of time) causes anxiety and encourages suspects to run or even fight with the police to elude capture. I'd argue arresting a suspect becomes unnecessary by deploying twenty-first century technology. Eliminate the need for arrest and eliminate the need to capture suspects, to book them or to temporarily house them.

During the court's business hours, after the suspect is booked, he is brought in front of a judge. This process is called an arraignment. In its simplest form, an arraignment is a procedure where the clerk reads off the charges and enters a plea of "not guilty" on the suspect's behalf. The judge arraigns him, and depending on his situation, the suspect is released until his next court date. At the arraignment, the suspect is issued a public defense attorney (if indigent) or retains his own attorney. Either way, he is released with his promise to appear at the next court date. The judge may inform the suspect of important procedural issues, such as his immigration status may be called into question if found guilty. The suspect is then deemed to have been arraigned. This all seems like a big waste of time.

The vast majority of district court cases are minor misdemeanors that include traffic or property crimes. Most often, the suspect is allowed to walk out the door after checking in with the probation department. In a handful of cases, the suspect is held by the judge to be sent to a correctional facility pending his next court date or for a dangerous hearing. However, this is the vast minority of cases. For every one-hundred arraignments, there may be one that is held in custody.

But what if a person is arrested after court business

hours? In Massachusetts, for example, after the booking process, the suspect is placed in a cell and the bail commissioner is notified. The bail commissioner looks over the details of the arrest, as well as the suspect's criminal history, and decides whether to post a bail or release them with nothing more than their promise to appear for arraignment. That means if the commissioner thinks the suspect will not appear in court on the next business day for arraignment, he can force the suspect to pay a bail. This amount is determined by the commissioner, and there are no hard and fast rules as to what amount is necessary. I've seen bails as low as two hundred dollars and as high as one hundred thousand dollars. If the suspect is able to retain the amount the commissioner dictates, he is released with his promise to appear on the date specified. The bail money is returned to the suspect only if he appears at the designated time.

This entire process seems like an unnecessary procedure if the suspect is a first-time offender or if there is no likelihood the arrestee will miss the arraignment. It's an exercise in futility. Why can't the officers on the street identify the suspect, determine who he is and release him with his promise to appear?

The need for police resources is therefore greatly

reduced (if not eliminated) if they are not tasked with transporting low-level prisoners to the station, booking them and subsequently bringing them to court. The steps I've introduced will bring society closer to eliminating the need for police altogether.

Police Reports

The most common type of victimization in America is property crime. I explore this issue in more depth in my book *Protect Yourself* (available on Amazon). The vast majority of property crime is stolen property, unattended car breaks or bank fraud. Many of these cases will never be solved due to the lack of evidence or lack of police follow-up. If, by chance, a police detective processes the victim's vehicle and discovers fingerprints of a suspect, they may locate and interview the suspect. Depending on what information is attained, the police may even charge someone with a crime. However, with the vast majority of cases, finding and lifting fingerprints from the interior of a car is impossible. This is most commonly due to the varying surfaces of a car's interior. However, even though most American communities have police departments who will dispatch a police officer to a victim's home, most will not dispatch a detective.

My solution is simple: instead of "deputizing" a few

select people (police officers) to take reports), the post-police era makes it everybody's responsibility to submit their own reports. Official crime reports will be submitted using the latest web-based portals. Gone are the days of a police officer coming to your home (making all the neighbors nervous at the sight of the black and white) and taking the pertinent information. The future of police reports is as simple as applying for a job on Indeed, the career website. Let's face it, the only reason a victim may file a police report is for insurance purposes. Most insurance providers will not take a claim of loss without the victim first filing a police report. You can't imagine how many people file a police report because they have lost their passport. Evidently, even the federal government will not replace it unless you've first reported it to the local cops.

If the loss is of a significantly small value, it will not be followed up by police anyway. Thus, police interaction is no longer necessary. In our new, online, self-reporting system, once the victim submits the pertinent information, along with cell phone pictures of damage, evidence, etc., a police administrator can review the file from a desk.

In some property theft incidents, the suspect is known to the victim. For example, I've seen cases where a "friend" steals medication from the victim's medicine cabinet (usually a painkiller). Today, the dispatch center receives a call about larceny and a police officer will take a report. He gathers the information, including the suspect's name, address, etc., and submit a report at the station. With this information, the officer will complete a court complaint application and request criminal charges against the suspect. However, in today's digital age, why can't the victim do this for themselves? In the post-police society, if the victim knows the thief, she can note the suspect's information in the self-initiated reporting system and submit a court complaint to the district court.

A common misconception is that the police "press charges" against a suspect. That is wrong. The police only make application to the court to have the person appear before a judge (as described earlier). This could include a summons, a clerk's hearing or an arrest warrant. Believe it or not, this is something any citizen can do in our current law enforcement system. In fact, in some unique circumstances, the police will recommend the citizen file their own application with the court. Thus, if this is the situation today, why can't it be implemented on a larger, universal scale? Why must we have a few gatekeepers of the criminal justice system when every American citizen is capable of making appropriate application to seek help from the court?

Unwanted Persons

One interesting incident in Brockton's call log from chapter four is the unwanted person call. I hypothesized that this was a homeless person sleeping or loitering on the property. I argue police response is not needed in this situation. Clearly, the homeless patron has every right to be in a public building. Oftentimes, citizens want undesirable people removed purely because of their unsightliness. This is a common issue in the winter when a homeless individual temporarily squats in an ATM vestibule. The fact that they are undesirable does not necessarily make them a criminal in need of police response. Library patrons and staff alike should be able to cohabitate with those whom they find "unwanted." Otherwise, it is upon the library staff to ask the gentleman to leave, not the police.

Medical Emergencies

The purpose of police officers responding to medical emergencies is based upon the theory that every second counts. Most American police officers are trained to give immediate life-saving support before the paramedics arrive. This is a policy that originated long before the modern-day advanced life support (ALS) paramedic existed. Not sixty years ago, local police departments were tasked with not only responding to health-related emergencies but also with loading patients into a station wagon police car and racing them to the hospital. Obviously, much has changed in the first responder field since then. Today, not only are paramedics trained in basic life support, but most communities employ advanced life support personnel.

As I described before, police officers are dispatched to medical emergencies to render first aid and CPR. Since patrol officers are on the road 24/7, they are able to respond quickly and to deploy life-saving measures. However, once highly trained paramedics arrive on the scene, the cops pull back and return to their traffic duties.

The usefulness of a police officer at medical emergency calls has ended. Rather than having a police officer respond, I propose communities hire additional paramedics at a fraction of the cost of a highly trained, full-time police officer. I suggest paramedics be taken out of ambulances and assigned to marked paramedic cruisers. Their limited and specific duty would be to arrive first at a medical emergency. It's less expensive to train and employ a paramedic than a full-time police officer, and they are more reliable on this type of call. Of course, an actual ambulance would also respond if the patient needs to be transported to the hospital.

However, under this system, the need for police has been eliminated.

This is just a small snapshot of what we as a society can implement to eliminate the need for police. If we evaluate different types of calls and what resources are actually required, we can achieve more and suffer less.

.

6. THE FUTURE WITHOUT POLICE

Just as I outlined in the previous chapters, much of what the police do is wasteful, time-consuming and laborious. Rather than focusing on enforcing the law, they've become inundated with trivial matters that go beyond the scope of their duties. A future without police is a future without police-involved shootings. Without citizens being gunned down or choked to death without cause at the hands of a brutal, oppressive force. According to *The Washington Post*, 992 people were shot and killed by the police in 2018. *The Post* has been collecting data on police-involved incidents since 2015; this data can be viewed on their website (https://www.washingtonpost.com/graphics/2019/national/police-shootings-2019/).

By deploying new technologies, society can maintain

the rule of law. Civilians will assume the role of police by filing their own reports, towing illegally parked vehicles, writing parking tickets, and issuing traffic violations. All these tasks can be satisfied in the post-police era by the use of surveillance cameras and other technology. Private security will secure property, paramedics will service medical emergency calls and administrators will review camera footage to enforce traffic guidelines and mailing citations. Federal administrators will be deployed to investigate serious crimes in local communities including murder, rape or armed, violent encounters. The public will remain just as safe as always, without violence and without the unsightliness of the uniformed police officer. What's more, the triggering effect by the sight of the police uniform will cease in the post-police era.

In the next chapter, I offer a dose of reality. Buckle up...

7. ARE YOU SERIOUS?

I apologize to those who may have been misled by the title of this book and found themselves nodding along to the arguments outlined in the previous chapters. Needless to say, there's no happy ending to this story. When I started this project, I tried to think of the most egregious argument to advocate for the abolishment of police. I then composed a list of police functions, and alongside each item, I listed the exact opposite. For every positive police function, I listed why that function was unnecessary. Although it went against every fiber of my being, I was able to make several somewhat realistic arguments to eliminate police service that even cops could support...maybe.

Much of what I've written in the previous chapters is unrealistic. However, there's no denying, there is another paradigm shift in American policing. The function of law enforcement is rapidly changing. Whether for the betterment of society or not, this change is inevitable. This paradigm shift coincides with the current state of recruitment in law enforcement agencies across the country. Many departments are struggling to fill vacancies to coincide with traditional staffing levels and the old style of policing. With the unappealing police job comes an impossible recruitment situation that will result in lower applicant turnout. Society will always have someone willing to follow an elephant with a shovel. Unfortunately, the candidate pool becomes ever more shallow when society discourages blue-collar occupations. Mike Rowe said it best, "In a very general way, our society has fallen out of love with the skilled trades. Part of the problem is a myriad of myths and misperceptions that surround the jobs themselves, but the biggest cause is our stubborn belief that a four-year degree is the best path for most people" (https://www.brainyquote.com/authors/mike-rowe-quotes).

When candidates apply to become police officers, the community hopes to get the best members of the community. Unfortunately, due to the anti-police rhetoric being spun by community and political leaders, it appears communities are just getting warm bodies to fill vacancies. I predict police departments will begin to shrink as the recruitment pool grows even shallower. With smaller police departments comes a reallocation of resources. Specialized units, such as community outreach programs, will be liquidated as officers are specifically tasked with law enforcement duties. Hence, quality-of-life complaints will go unheeded. Gone are the days of police officers responding to parking complaints, dogs off leashes, fire alarms, medical emergencies and conducting building checks. The role of the police officer is reduced out of areas that are either unrelated or beyond the reasonable scope of their duties.

In chapter four, I outlined several police calls for service in Brockton that could have been mitigated over the phone or handled by civilian specialists. Examples include dispatching meter maids for parking complaints, utilizing security surveillance cameras to check public buildings or animal complaints being serviced by civilian animal personnel. As I mentioned in an earlier chapter, hiring first-responder sub-contractors has already begun with paramedics. Emergency life support sub-contractors provide better trained professionals and better equipment without the scheduling hassles or expensive employee benefits. The municipality pays the private company a weekly fee and service is provided.

Another example is in-house information technology (IT) services. Since police information is sensitive, departments historically assign sworn police officers to protect the intelligence. However, as law enforcement adopts technology, local towns are subcontracting their IT departments to private entities. Why would someone have to become a cop first to provide IT services? It's a waste of resources. The wider use of body-cams being used by police agencies across the country is creating a digital storage nightmare for local communities. Unfortunately, the software and equipment also requires a large amount of attention to maintain. The software must be constantly updated as technology changes. The equipment is being worn forty, sixty, sometimes eighty times a week. Like any other piece of police equipment, it gets dropped, banged and broken. This equipment needs constant attention that most law enforcement agencies do not have the manpower to provide. Thus, body-cam companies are spreading faster than any other equipment industry in the history of policing.

Although I do not ascribe to all the items I have previously outlined, I do propose a new crime-focused approach to policing. Under a new, reduced-task approach, departments will need a smaller sworn staff focused specifically on enforcing the law and investigating criminal activity. All other non-law enforcement activity can be farmed to other municipal departments and private sub-contractors.

8 THE FUTURE OF POLICING

I wrote a chapter on the future of policing in my 2016 book *#Nationwide Police Strike*. At the time, I contended the future of policing was to adopt the community policing model from the 90s era. I was wrong. As we progress further and further into anti-police lunacy, I'm convinced the future of policing is both dismal and terrifying. First, police officers of tomorrow will become the generalists of society. Police departments will be forced to address trivial matters as opposed to focusing on emergency criminal justice response. We'll drift even further away from the idyllic approach to law enforcement, which is enforcing the laws set forth by the local community, state or federal government.

As we do today, the local route cop will answer any nonsense complaint that travels over Thomas Edison's phone lines. No matter whether its rotten food in the refrigerator, trouble finding a parking space at Walmart or a depressed teen on a Friday night, the police will be called. The officer will respond to appease and mitigate the situation, no matter how trivial it may seem.

This type of nanny state policing has already begun. An example of this is emergency calls for a prepubescent teenager who refuses to go to school. Imagine that? A parent who can't parent their kid calls the police because the kid refuses to go to school. I've personally responded to many calls just like this. The officer is obligated to respond and try their best to persuade little Johnny to stop playing video games and attend school. What's more, civilian dispatchers are being instructed that they no longer have the ability to filter out these needless calls. Evidently, dispatchers lack the mental fortitude to decipher whether a police response is appropriate. Thus, they're directed to send a cop no matter how ridiculous.

This alternate universe is a situation police agencies have brought upon themselves. Over the past few years municipalities and police departments have relinquished control to an anti-cop society by pandering to the most vocal of agitators. In an effort to appease the extremists, the top brass in the police department essentially told street cops they were the problem. By doing their job and fulfilling their obligation, individual police officers we're told they've created this hostile environment. To defend their actions, municipalities cite the officers' inherent biases, toxic masculinity and dangerous microaggressions that have besieged American law enforcement agencies. They shout procedural justice is the answer without any clear definition of what that consists of.

As you'll read in the following Case Studies chapter, a good example of this is Daniel Pantaleo, who was recently fired from the NYPD. Instead of addressing the disease, police administrators subject street cops to hours of additional training to illuminate the officers to their inherent bias and inadvertent racism. Apparently, all cops have an underlying level of severe racism that can't be ignored by liberal do-gooders.

Over the years, American police departments have responded to various outcries by changing their main objective from enforcing laws to forging relationships with the community. Several national attempts of the relationship-forging function have gained popularity in recent years. The most universally known is Coffee with a Cop (CWC). This program was unofficially erected in Hawthorne, California, in 2011, and it spread like wildfire. Programs like Coffee with a Cop sound great. How could anybody be against the idea of communities partnering for the common good? Nobody. However, what we soon learned was officers who volunteered were commonly met with sideways glances and several layers of a "better than you" attitude. Unfortunately, every CWC event contained one citizen who consumed the officers' time with complaints about speeding cars or the neighbor's barking dog. Obviously, this was not the purpose of this program. Forging relationships is about interacting with another human on a personal level. CWC events were intended to have the cop engage about the weather and local events and connect on a human level. The purpose was to not hear a laundry list of complaints.

As a result of the negative press the last couple years, regular people have become triggered by the sight of the police uniform. Unfortunately, in the course of their day, people don't want to see cops. Several years ago, I was sitting in a nearly vacant parking lot eating my lunch in my police cruiser. I was approached by a woman who identified herself as a local resident and asked what I was doing. With my mouth full of ham and cheese, I motioned to my sandwich (clearly indicating I was *fishing*). She politely requested I find another place to eat so as not to concern the neighbors. Ugh.

Unfortunately, there are thousands of examples like this every day. Cops bite their tongue and move along like good public servants.

Cops should not exist to "concern" or be a burden to neighbors. However, this is the direction we're heading. The simple answer is to minimize the number of uniformed police officers assigned to any geographic area. In an easily triggered society, the elimination of the police uniform is the only option to prevent snowflake anxiety. To attempt to explain the uniform triggering paradox, we need to review the history of the modern-day police uniform. The purpose of a police officer wearing easily distinguishable clothing was to act as a visible deterrent to criminal activity. The theory was criminals would be less likely to commit a crime if the neighborhood was crawling with cops. This has worked for the last 200 years. However, since the type of crime being committed has changed over the years, the purpose of the uniform has become obsolete. Less opportunity crime is being reported. Opportunity crime is defined as one that is committed when the opportunity presents itself. A classic example is the vagrant breaking into an unsecured home or stealing from an unlocked parked car. What's more, violent street robberies have been almost eradicated in the United States. Without street crimes and in-progress opportunity crimes, cops' primary function has become nonsense calls like little Johnny playing hooky. Every minute of a cop's time is committed to hopping from one needless service call to the next, giving the uniform no time to act as a deterrent.

As we've seen from chapter four, the average police department only gets a handful of true emergency calls on any given day. When they arrive on a hot call, their uniform easily distinguishes them from everybody else as they service the call. However, how many of these uniforms do police departments need patrolling the street? Some would argue policing in the future will require two or three uniformed police officers to answer the emergencies and the rest in plain, street clothes to answer non-emergency calls. This approach would save the easily triggered public from the sight of the uniform and not raise concern while we eat our ham and cheese sandwich.

9. CASE STUDIES

Brockton, MA: On August 21st, 2019 a man visited a Brockton, Massachusetts, electronic store in an attempt to return a recently purchased cell phone. When the employee informed him that he could take the phone back, the customer became upset. Surveillance video from inside the store shows the man flailing his arms and breaking merchandise. He then reached into his gym bag and pulled out a hatchet. He began swinging the hatchet at the items on the counter and across the counter at the store employees.

A uniformed police officer who was assisting with a funeral procession was flagged down by a witness who observed the activity in the store. The police officer broke from his assignment and sprang into action, entering a very violent situation. After several requests to put the hatchet down, the man lunged at the officer with the hatchet. The officer discharged his weapon and neutralized the threat (i.e., shot him in the chest).

It's no coincidence that I chose to highlight the fine police work by the Brockton Police Department. Since they were the guinea pigs of chapter four, I used their heroics to illustrate a need for constant police presence. This case demonstrates why it's important to have a widespread dispersal of uniformed police officers. Any delay in police response may have resulted in further damage to property, injury or death to an innocent bystander. The witness who alerted the officer was able to easily identify him by his marked police cruiser and distinguishable uniform, thus saving valuable time with an immediate response by Brockton Police.

New York, NY: Daniel Pantaleo was a police officer for the NYPD. He grew up in Staten Island and was trained in the police academy in 2006. He was a proactive cop, making over 300 arrests in his short career. He was eventually assigned to a special unit tasked with addressing quality-of-life issues by enforcing street crime. On July 17, 2014, he and other officers responded to a disturbance in front of a beauty shop in his hometown. While investigating the issue, one of the officers recognized a man by the name of Eric Garner whom Pantaleo previously knew to be involved in criminal activity. The officers suspected he was selling "loosie" cigarettes on the street, which of course is a crime. When one of the officers engaged Garner, he became uncooperative and evasive. He mentioned how he was tired of being harassed and declared it "ends today."

When the decision was made to place Garner under arrest, he began to resist the officers' instructions and lawful authority to take him into custody. As a result, Officer Pantaleo put Garner into a hold where his arm wrapped around his neck. The officers were intending to take Garner to the ground to control and handcuff him. The police supervisor on scene called for an ambulance after Garner complained he was having trouble breathing. Garner was alive when the paramedics placed him on a stretcher and loaded him into the ambulance. Garner died of a heart attack on his way to the hospital. Most people upset with Garner's untimely demise should have focused on the ineptitude of the FDNY paramedics for not providing Garner oxygen or attaching a defibrillator to monitor Garner's heart rhythm. However, the outrage was directed at the easier anti-cop target: Officer Pantaleo and the NYPD.

Following a criminal investigation of Officer Daniel

Pantaleo by local authorities, the case was presented to a grand jury for criminal indictment. To the surprise of local leaders and the cop-hating mob, the grand jury decided not to file criminal charges against the officer. What's more, five years later, Attorney General Bill Barr announced Panteleo would not face Federal Department of Justice criminal charges.

Daniel Pantaleo was fired on August 19, 2019, from the NYPD.

The point of this case study is to illustrate the volatility of the police occupation. There was a time when police officers were trained in the academy to win, no matter what. If a suspect resisted or showed violent force, the new officer was taught to take control of the situation and deploy any means necessary to effectively do their job. Those days are over. The forces of modern-day society are training police officers to lose. They're being taught it's better to give up than to be labeled a racist cop who killed a person of color. Essentially, the mob tells them to take a couple hits to the face before deploying any amount of force. Otherwise, the officer will be unemployed and face criminal charges like Daniel Pantaleo.

So, what's the only reasonable response for the officer who faces this cognitive struggle? The answer is simply to do nothing. Become reactive. Do not place yourself into a situation where you're required to deploy defensive tactics. At the same time, make it appear as if you're doing your job.

I equate this reactionary function to the fire department. When was the last time you saw a fire engine patrolling the street looking for a fire to extinguish? Never. Because of cases like Daniel Pantaleo, the modern-day profession of policing will eventually become solely reactive. Police will take no proactive steps to stop criminal activity and only become engaged if dispatched to a call. This is not the right direction of policing in America. Criminals must be kept at bay by constant fear of being found and caught by the cops. This is the only true way to protect people from becoming victimized.

10. CONCLUSION

Following the release of my Amazon best seller *#Nationwide Police Strike*, I was the victim of a keyboard attack by "woke" activists. The local Facebook community in the community where I'm employed as a police officer became unglued because I dared to voice my adverse opinion. To them, I was a mere brainless, civil-servant who could not compete with the wit of faceless lunatics. Many hid behind the shield of social media equipped with virtual pitchforks and torches. The mob eventually called for my badge. As it would happen, many elected officials of the town were listening intently and called upon the police chief to take action. It was an unpleasant time for myself and my family who watched closely for the outcome. Luckily, common sense triumphed, and the troublemakers who began the march toward lunacy were silenced. The brass for whom I work defended my first amendment right to speak my mind. It should be noted that in *#Nationwide Police Strike*, just as in this book, I never identified my employing community, nor in any way indicated that my ideas or opinions reflected my police department. Nonetheless, the proverbial "mad" cat was let out of the bag.

I cringe at the thought that for a short time, I may have contributed to the already stressful job of my chief of police. That is the very last thing I'd ever want to do. But at the end of the day, he sided with common sense, dignity and resolve. He is a good man, and he was a great chief.

I would like to think this op-ed book will not meet the same fate. I considered keeping this project to myself in the interest of not making waves; however, that would represent surrender. Allowing the mob to attack my work, my opinion and my character with impunity is equivalent to declaring defeat. A great man once said, "I will not be defeated...I will compromise, and I will negotiate, but defeat?" I will be knocked down, demoralized and branded a lesser human because of my outspoken opinion, but it won't silence me. As an American first and a police officer second, I will not be denied my first amendment rights because they happen to be unpopular with a vocal few. I should have the same medium by which to voice my opinions as anybody else and given neither more nor less legitimacy because of my occupation.

As I stated in the introduction, this work is mine. The opinions expressed in the preceding pages do not represent my employer, my family, my cats or the goat I rented to eat the poison ivy in my yard. These opinions are of a sound mind and will not be suppressed.

I will not be defeated.

1. INTRODUCTION

The purpose of law is to dictate behavior. Behavior is modified by creating law and by threatening punishment. Contrary to popular belief, the function of any governing body is not social programs, infrastructure, entitlements or even financial stability. The government's primary function is to keep its inhabitants safe. Protection is above all else. Governments, both federal and local, motivate citizens to voluntarily comply with rules of order for fear of being held accountable. This may consist of losing a convenient privilege, like driving a car, or loss of liberties, like jail. The earliest record of law from Ancient Egypt, around 3000 BC. A Sumerian king by the name of Ur-

Nammu created a code of laws that consisted of over thirty rules banishing violence and strife, among other things. Several centuries later, his successor King Hammurabi reduced these laws to writing by inscribing them onto tablets. Hammurabi displayed several of these stones throughout his kingdom as warnings to those who violated them. Not much has changed in five thousand years. Humans from every corner of the planet create rules for their people to follow and hold those accountable who do not. As citizens of our perspective, geographic areas, we cannot choose which rules we want to follow. Of course, you wouldn't know that by watching mainstream media in 2020.

Laws are made to protect people. Simple. One should be safe shopping at the grocery store without fear of being robbed, beaten or otherwise harmed. Alternatively, humans should not feel the need to prey on other humans. For the most part, that works. My mother and father taught me at a young age to respect other people and to resist the urge to steal, burn and loot. "Do not cause mayhem for mayhem's sake." I was actually never told that, but I was clever enough to figure that out on my own.

As our faith in humankind becomes lost in the smoke of digital popularity, our common decency goes along with it. The younger generation in 2020 seems to be more preoccupied in becoming a YouTube star than in being a productive member of society. They take no ownership in the destructive action their viral videos cause. How many videos have we seen on social media where a victim required help, but our YouTube videographer was too busy getting it on tape? Oftentimes, his own narration will recognize the fact he should be helping the old lady but elects to maintain his angle shot instead.

When common decency is lost, the government is forced to enact rules for people to follow to maintain order and to protect its citizens. What's more, the government needs other humans to enforce the laws they've created. Enter law enforcement officers. The government seeks the finest individuals of society to detect crime and to catch law-breakers. Once arrested, the criminal is brought to court. The court seeks justice, and the person is punished according to their crime.

But what happens when leaders of that society no longer want the law to be enforced? What if law-makers decide it's acceptable for its people to violate certain laws? Or better yet, what if they advocate for their constituents to refuse to follow certain laws, while dehumanizing, delegitimizing and disregarding those who are tasked with enforcing the law? Then you have the summer of 2020.

I don't want to overstate the issue, but before reading the argument laid out in this book, I want the reader to comprehend the current disposition of local police officers. This year, municipal and city police officers nationwide have taken quite a beating. The uniform and government-issued authority have made cops an easy target for the privileged millennial. They climb from mom's basement with dark clothing and black umbrellas and search for a badge to attack. When these social justice warriors are caught pushing the envelope a little too far, their defense calls themselves "protesters." What a world.

Understandably, this has caused an incredible strain on police departments' recruiting efforts. If you thought there were recruitment problems following the incidents in Fergusson, Missouri, or in Baltimore, Maryland, how about adding nonstop riots across the country, threats to defund police organizations and unrelenting abuse from average everyday citizens? That seems like an unpleasant environment for a human. What's worse, those who are currently employed by police officers are packing up their lockers and heading for the exit. Good luck with all that recruitment stuff!

In my book *Abolish the Police,* I discussed recruitment issues facing law enforcement agencies long before a crooked Minneapolis cop murdered a man over counterfeiting:

When candidates apply to become police officers, the community hopes to get the best members of the community. Unfortunately, due to the anti-police rhetoric being spun by community and political leaders, it appears communities are just getting warm bodies to fill vacancies. I predict police departments will begin to shrink as the recruitment pool grows even more shallow. With smaller police departments comes a reallocation of resources. Specialized units, such as community outreach programs, will be liquidated as officers will be specifically tasked with law enforcement duties. Hence, quality-of-life complaints will go unheeded. Gone are the days of police officers responding to parking complaints, dogs off leashes, fire alarms, medical emergencies and conducting building checks. The role of the police officer is reduced to areas that are either unrelated or beyond the reasonable scope of their duties.

This is the future of American policing. I, for one, welcome the change. Police departments have been overpriced conglomerates who seek only to violate the rights of others (sarcasm stressed). Several local elected officials have even called for "leaner" police departments (whatever that means) or to outrageously defund them altogether. This is the very essence of *Abolish the Police*. Lawmakers are essentially telling the working-class citizen that they're on their own. This is the result of their insane proposals.

So, why federalize the police? Could disbanding local law enforcement in lieu of a federal police force benefit the public? The public may not even have an option. The federal government may be forced to step in when the local establishment refuses to take crime and public safety seriously. Take, for example, June 26, 2020: the Minneapolis City Council voted unanimously to alter the city's charter to allow for the police department to be dismantled. What then? Will they rely on the Minnesota State Police, who are barely equipped to cover the roadways, to assume the burden of policing a major metropolitan area? If you live in the greater Minneapolis area, you should be very concerned for your safety. Ironically, "the city of Minneapolis has paid two private security firms $63,000 over the last three weeks to protect three City Council members," after they voted to abolish their police department, according to the *Minneapolis StarTribune* article dated June 30, 2020. Thus, taxpayers can fund the physical security of the elite, but not for everyone else.

What if more cities follow this lead? Who will go running in when everyone is running out? By the end of this book, you should be able to answer this question. My hope is you have a better understanding of the volatility of a society without a neighborhood police department.

Disclaimer: This book was written by a cop. I'm pro-law enforcement, pro-America, pro-second amendment and anti-anarchy. I was raised to follow the rules and understand the difference between right and wrong. I believe in God and subscribe to the teachings of Jesus Christ. If any of these declarations bother you, I would not continue reading. I'd put this book down and find something else to do...I won't judge.

Remember this: At the end of each chapter, you'll find a chapter summary labelled *"Remember this."* The information contained in this small paragraph is the biggest takeaway from the chapter. If you remember nothing else from this book, remember these summaries.

2. TYPES OF LAW

There are three levels of government responsible for enacting and enforcing law. These bodies can be best described as ranging from micro to macro. Micro represents the local city or township where macro is the federal law. As stated in the previous chapter, the general idea of any law is to establish and to maintain civil obedience. Laws discourage and prevent crimes by removing violators from society. We'll review these levels of government and how they apply to the common man.

Federal Law

Federal law tends to be broader to cover crimes that affect the safety of the country. Laws passed by U.S. Congress are used to address a federal or national issue. Federal law must remain broad and consistent to apply types of geographic areas. For example, it has to be applicable for Texas as well as Alaska. Thus, federal law is kept broad by design. Laws passed by U.S. Congress are used to address a federal or national issue. For example, federal code establishes immigration law to prevent illegal entry into the United States. This is an awesome responsibility that small border towns like El Paso, Texas, do not have the resources to address. The federal government has thousands of law enforcement officers specifically trained and equipped to address these laws.

Creating and enforcing federal law makes total sense to me. What makes no sense is when people attempt to obstruct the enforcement of laws in the name of politics. For example, in 2017, some American groups called to abolish the Immigration and Customs Enforcement (ICE) agency. They claimed enforcing this type of law was racist. A well-known freshman congresswoman made it her rallying cry in the name of social justice. She single-handedly motivated like-minded sheep to attack

ICE facilities and ICE officers. If this congresswoman had any sense of how the process works, she could have introduced legislation and altered the Patriot Act (the law that created ICE). But instead, she used her position to manipulate her army of basement dwellers. We were right to ignore them.

State Law

Next is state law. Many states enact laws to protect their residents with region-specific rules. For example, Massachusetts has many laws that govern the way Gloucester fisherman conduct business (Gloucester is a north shore fishing town made famous by the movie *The Perfect Storm*). Of course, these laws would be useless in the landlocked state of Tennessee. States pass these laws with the understanding that state-sworn police officers will enforce them. I'm always amused by states that impose stricter laws than their neighbors. Take for example the helmet law. Massachusetts has a strict helmet law while its neighbor to the north (New Hampshire) has none. The way I see it, most public safety laws are designed to protect the unsuspecting victim from injury. Serious offenses like murder, rape, and robbery are all designed to protect the innocent.

Speed limits and other minor motor vehicle rules protect Mrs. Jones from Johnny and his Camaro.

But other than the operator of the motorcycle (who chooses not to wear one), who does the helmet law protect? If motorcycle Willy loses control and meets a stone wall, is Willy's helmetless head hurting anybody but Willy? Is the unsightliness of Willy's hair enough to mandate a protective barrier between his skull and the pavement? Or, is the helmet law just another example of big-brother knowing what's best for its minions? Aren't the serfs smart enough in Massachusetts to decide for themselves whether helmets are right for them?

Some may argue consumption of controlled substances falls into this category as well, but I disagree. Unlike helmets, drugs carry crime and other quality-of-life issues that affect society. The helmet law is in a class all by itself, and frankly, I'm tired of the government dictating what's right for me. If Willy and I want our hair flowing in the wind just before mortal impact, so be it!

Local Law

On the micro level of our discussion, each
community passes its own by-laws or city
ordinances depending on the community's form of
government. Town by-laws can cover everything
from building permits to motor vehicle violations.
Local police and town officials are tasked with
enforcing passed laws by issuing civil citations to
maintain compliance. Littering laws, for example,
are used to maintain clean streets. Oftentimes,
these laws are enacted to appease a small faction
of the vocal complainers at the expense of law-
abiding residents. Case in point: towns in
Massachusetts have enacted laws designed to curb
the use of leaf blowers. Advocates use climate
change emissions or noise disturbances to justify it.
But normal people see it for what it really is:
pandering to a few losers who have nothing better
to do than complain about their neighbors. Local
cops are forced to write monetary citations for
observed violations that do nothing but cause a
divide between the police and the public.

Court

Once a criminal law is deemed to have been broken, the individual is taken into custody for the purposes of identification and to be brought before a judge. In my book *Abolish the Police,* I go into significant detail with regard to the arrest process. If you haven't read that book, I highly recommend it! The arrestee is brought to a district or federal court depending upon the law enforcement agency that effected the arrest. In some instances when the court is closed, the arrestee will be released after posting a monetary bail. The money posted by the arrestee is returned once he shows up for court, or the case is otherwise adjudicated. Since people don't like to forfeit money, this is a surefire way to get defendants to show up for court. Although this system has worked for hundreds of years, some see the bail process as class warfare. For example, in January 2020, the state of New York decided this monetary requirement was unfair to those who have none, so now criminals must be released after arrest and arraignment (if possible). This law was subsequently amended in April 2020, to allow for judges to impose bail for some offenses. New Jersey and California have passed similar laws, but nothing as radical as New York.

Whether the arrestee is released by bail or held for court, the individual is required to eventually appear before a judge. If the arrestee refuses to follow the conditions dictated by the court, he can be brought to a county jail until trial. This procedure applies to both federal and state courts. In some instances, one who violates a town by-law (or city ordinance) can be arrested; however, the officer must prove that the person willfully disregarded the by-law. This is achieved by issuing the individual a citation and catching them committing a subsequent offense again. By-law arrests, however, are usually adjudicated by nothing more than a stern warning from the judge.

Remember this: there are all types of laws that regulate all types of behavior. The commonality between each level of government is its duty to protect its people by the issuance and enforcement of laws.

3. LOCAL MUNICIPAL POLICE

Policing in America originated as a means of protecting colonial farmers from thieves. Apparently, criminals were sneaking onto farms in the middle of the night to steal chickens. The farmer would hire a local to watch his farm so he could sleep. This eventually developed into a more serious vocation as communities began to grow.

In the early 20th century, full-time sheriffs were hired to enforce recently passed laws and to maintain order. Unfortunately, officers were hired without much training preceding the job. The applicant had to be big and tough enough to fight off the local chicken thief. As recently as the 1970s, police training was limited to only a couple of weeks. This training consisted primarily of current state law and department policy (if they had one).

A recently retired cop told me when he was hired in the mid-1970s, the department gave him a uniform and a gun and told him to "hit the streets." After several months, he attended a four-week police academy.

We've come a long way in the last forty years with respect to policing in America. When I attended the police academy in 2001, the focus was physical fitness, police procedures and defensive tactics. Every day, the staff drove home the idea that "you'll do whatever it takes to survive" and to never give up when you're in "the fight." They taught us what force was permitted under certain circumstances and how to protect ourselves while servicing calls. We were told we would see shit that would cause permanent memory burn—blood, death and evil that would make the average person lose their lunch. The academy instructors showed pictures of horrific and gruesome crime scenes. One instructor asked the class, "If you can't stomach a photograph, how will you be able to handle it in real life?"

Fast forward twenty years, when every human on

the planet has a video camera in their pocket. For the first time, the public is able to see firsthand what cops see every day. Understandably, these images scare the shit out of them. Ironically, many of the viral videos on social media show tactically sound responses by the cops. Most only show only a portion of the incident. The cops use approved techniques that follow training guidelines, and they are able to get the job done. Sometimes, the outcome is disturbing to watch, but upon review, the cop did everything right. The snowflake generation needs to get a grip and wait to pass judgment. Just because something looks awful does not necessarily mean it was wrong. Of course, the flipside is also true. I've watched many videos that caused me to shake my head and ask, "What the hell was that cop thinking?"

An appropriate example of an appropriate police response happened in my own police department in 2017. Dispatch received a call for an in-progress breaking-and-entering where the suspect smashed through the front door. Minutes before he forced his way into the occupied home, he rang the bell, which is a common tactic by residential burglars to assure the home is vacant.

Not expecting any visitors, the lone victim didn't bother looking out the window. Thus, when nobody answered the door, the burglar smashed a six-inch decorative window along the border of the entryway. He reached through the broken glass and unlocked the deadbolt from inside. Once he overcame his biggest obstacle, he was ready for his looting spree. However, upon hearing the smashing glass, the elderly resident scooted out the back door and called 9-1-1 from her cell. Three uniformed patrol units (including myself) were there in seconds. When one of the officers confronted the burglar in the dining room, he spun on his heels and dove head-first through the dining room window. The officer who witnessed Jimmy-the-Superfly move couldn't believe his eyes. To those of us outside, the sound of his body slamming into the glass sounded like an explosion. Needless to say, the criminal was busted. He fought with us outside for a moment but was still too stunned by his leap of death to put up any kind of meaningful struggle. To anybody watching, it may have looked as though the cops roughed this guy up in the alley. Had an observer not seen the dummy jump through the plate glass window, the viral video would've led to riots in the streets. By watching only the video, the mob would wrongly assume the cops were responsible for his head trauma and bloody face. Failure to look at the totality of the circumstances causes knee-jerk reactions that usually turn into inappropriate actions.

Remember this: those who are tasked with enforcing those rules have an awesome responsibility to be fair and professional. Failure to do so will result in negative consequences for the officer and the agency. However, selling a false narrative and using law enforcement as a scapegoat for political purposes also has consequences. Municipal police agencies may be reaching that breaking point.

4. FEDERAL LAW ENFORCEMENT

There are many arms of law enforcement that report to the federal government. Sometimes affectionately referred to as alphabet agencies, they all have their own particular responsibilities. For example, border patrol protects both our northern and southern borders (as well as other ports of entry) from illegal crossings. That's a very specific function with a very specific protocol for officers to follow. The laws they enforce may be similar to other agencies like Immigration and Customs Enforcement but are substantially different from agencies like the Environmental Protection Agency. This chapter will identify and summarize the duties of the seven largest and most familiar federal law enforcement agencies.

FBI

The most familiar agency under the federal law enforcement umbrella is the Federal Bureau of Investigations. The FBI is responsible for investigating a whole host of national criminal activity. This includes terrorism, cybercrime, public corruption, civil rights, white-collar and organized crime. According to their website (fbi.gov), their mission is "to protect the American people and uphold the Constitution of the United States."

An example of their work includes the July 29, 2020, arrest of a University of Arkansas professor named Simon Saw-Teong Ang. Evidently, Ang was indicted by a federal grand jury in the Western District of Arkansas on forty-two counts of wire fraud and passport fraud. While employed by the University of Arkansas, the professor and researcher was receiving compensation from the communist country of China while receiving U.S. government grants. This agreement violated the conflict of interest law to which Ang was subsequently arrested and charged.

Obviously, not the hard hitting, sensational stories of Agents Moulder and Scully from the Fox television show *The X-files*, but critical law enforcement none-the-less.

ATF

The Alcohol, Tobacco and Firearms agency is a law enforcement agency specifically geared to addressing specific, namesake violations. According to their website (atf.gov), the "ATF is a law enforcement agency in the United States Department of Justice that protects our communities from violent criminals, criminal organizations, the illegal use and trafficking of firearms, the illegal use and storage of explosives, acts of arson and bombings, acts of terrorism, and the illegal diversion of alcohol and tobacco products." A little more exciting than their white-collar counterparts at the FBI and not dissimilar from your typical, municipal police officer.

In recent years, their duties have expanded to include investigating arson and explosives. With these added responsibilities, the ATF has been involved in several major incidents including the Oklahoma City bombing in 1995 and the September 11, 2001 tragedy.

The ATF is most remembered for their involvement in the 1993 raid on David Koresh and his Branch Davidians compound in Waco, Texas. Along with the FBI, the ATF was tasked with executing federal warrants on February 28, 1993. Under the orders of then Secretary of State Janet Reno and the Clinton Administration, ATF agents visited the compound to serve a search warrant. They were met with gunfire from within the compound that killed four agents and wounded dozens more. The federal agents pulled back, which began a 51-day standoff between cult members and the police. The cease-fire came to a crashing halt when one of the buildings mysteriously caught on fire. According to the ATF, agents were forced to deploy tear gas to get the inhabitants out of the burning building. Nobody really knows what really exchanged between cult members and federal agents other than it will remain in history as a complete debacle.

DEA

Much like the ATF, the Drug Enforcement Agency (DEA) is geared to enforcing large-scale drug crimes. In the summer of 2020, DEA agents worked with local law enforcement to identify and track the movements of two dozen criminals as they moved heroin, methamphetamine and fentanyl across the border and into California. They tracked the drugs as they were divided and distributed by a network of dealers and pushers. On July 28, the Seattle, WA DEA division office released a media alert reporting, "Fifteen people were arrested today throughout the Puget Sound region and in California following an 18-month investigation of a drug trafficking organization tied to the CJNG cartel in Mexico."

USSS

The United States Secret Service was originally created to investigate United States currency forgery. Originally, American banks printed their own "bank notes" that one would exchange for goods and services. In 1863, the U.S. began issuing national bank notes in response to states' varying levels of inflation of their notes during the Civil

War. Several southern states excessively produced and distributed southern currency to raise money to fight the north. This of course caused the value of certain notes to plummet in value. Shortly after a national currency was created, the United States Secret Service agency was created to assure counterfeiting was detected and enforced. By 1867, their duties broadened to investigate additional frauds against the government including fraudulent land deals, fraudulent distilleries and even terrorist groups like the Ku Klux Klan. Most of these responsibilities were delegated to newer federal law enforcement agencies with those specific duties.

However, following the assassination of President William McKinley in 1901, the agency assumed the awesome responsibility of protecting the commander-in-chief. This is the task the agency is best known for today. However, with the advent and commercialization of digital commerce, the Secret Service has again broadened its responsibilities to investigate cybercrimes that target U.S. financial institutions and critical infrastructure.

Most recently, the US Secret Service charged a Detroit (Michigan) woman for her role in a multi-million dollar unemployment insurance fraud scheme. During the COVID-19 pandemic, she and her team of criminals cheated the State of Michigan and the U.S. Government by exploiting emergency unemployment assistance. The suspect was a contractor for the state's insurance office who fraudulently released COVID-19 relief funds to people who neither qualified nor applied for assistance.

What's unique to the Secret Service is the agency also has a uniformed component. While the common image of a secret service agent is in a suit and tie and sunglasses, their uniform is not very dissimilar from your local police department. Unlike the FBI, ATF or DEA, the USSS has a division specifically tasked with protecting the White House, the Vice President's residence and the treasury department property in Washington D.C. The uniform division of the Secret Service is probably the most comparable to a municipal police department. In addition to uniforms, the secret service is also equipped with patrol cars, motorcycles, and civil disturbance equipment, and it is trained to respond to all sorts of service calls. For example, in February, 2016, uniformed Secret Service officers were hailed heroes after providing first aid to a man in a federal building. By responding quickly and professionally, uniformed secret service agents were able to administer CPR and save the man's life. Equipped with lifesaving tools and training, the Secret Service mirrors the work of local cops.

US Postal Police

The postal police, now called United States Postal Inspectors, is an agency tasked with deterring and investigating mail crimes. Boasting their jurisdiction as worldwide, "the Postal Inspection Service enforces over 200 federal statutes related to crimes that involve the postal system, its employees, and its customers" (uspis.gov). This includes crimes such as postal fraud, dangerous items sent through the mail, cybercriminals that target the mail system and even securing USPS assets during natural disasters.

What's interesting about the US Postal Police is

their organized deployment. Unlike the Secret Service Uniformed Division, who are primarily assigned to Washington D.C., the Postal Police have offices in every major city in America. Their inspectors and uniform personnel can deploy to any local post office in a matter of minutes. The postal police divide the country into nine different zones, including the Northeast; New York Metro area; Eastern; CAP Metro area; Southeast; Great Lakes; Western; Southwest; and Pacific. Each area has a hierarchy of staff from the police director (a.k.a chief of police) to uniformed patrol officers. As I'll explain in a future chapter, a similar organizational structure should be used to deploy a federal police force.

The Postal Police were integral in investigating and capturing a man named Ted Kaczynski. Between 1976 and 1996, the *Unabomber*, which he was affectionately called, sent 16 explosive devices through the mail. A team of FBI, ATF and Postal Police Agents were formed with the specific duty to seek and apprehend him. It wasn't until Kaczynski mailed a letter he wanted published to a newspaper that he was apprehended. The Postal Inspection officers were the key agency involved in this case.

Amtrak Police

Most people don't realize Amtrak has its own police department. Amtrak established the authority to have its own police force with the Rail Passenger Service Act of 1970, which is now found at Federal code 49 U.S.C. 24101. Although Amtrak defines itself as a "for-profit corporation," their relationship with the state and federal government is mutually dependent. The board of directors that run the corporation rely on the federal government for the railways. However complicated the railway transportation system is, the Amtrak police is not.

Amtrak police receive their police powers not only by the federal government but by city and state laws. Thus, officers have the same legal authority as a local or state law enforcement officer within their jurisdiction. They are trained by the Federal Law Enforcement Training Centers (FLETC) not unlike their municipal or state police counterparts. The main focus of deployment is trains and Amtrak property, such as stations and other infrastructure.

Like the Postal Inspection Police, Amtrak Police
Department divides the country into six geographic
locations. These include New England; Mid-Atlantic
North; Mid-Atlantic South; New York Metro;
Central and Western. Thus, it is another example of
a national deployment of uniformed police patrol
services that is key to successful federal law
enforcement.

ICE

It is the duty of the Immigration and Customs
Enforcement (ICS) agency to address issues of
people illegally entering the United States. This
agency was formed shortly after the September 11,
2001, attacks on the World Trade Center in New
York and on the Pentagon in Washington D.C. The
Patriot Act of 2002 combined the U.S. Customs
Service and Immigration and Naturalization Service
(INS), forming the agency we know today as ICE.
Following a 9/11 investigation, we learned these
agencies monitored the same people on a daily
basis, and it was only natural that these two
agencies became one. In addition, the operational
goal of both agencies was to maintain control over

individuals coming into the country and to prevent another heinous attack. In fact, the absence of a major terrorist attack in America is a testament that the system truly works.

In the hectic, anti-Tump climate of 2018/2019, the Immigration and Custom Enforcement (ICE) agency came under heavy rebuke. Because of disagreements in the manner in which immigration law was being enforced, ICE became the focus of the left's anger. An example was a Portland, Oregon ICE facility that came under physical attack. This "occupy" group was able to shut down the operations of this field office for a short time. The following summer, a man was killed by ICE agents when he crashed the Tacoma, Washington, ICE detention center equipped with a rifle and several incendiary devices.

Needless to say, the attacks by several congressmen in Washington had a profound response by locals in metropolitan areas. What's ironic is ICE officials are only allowed to enforce laws created and passed by congress. Thus, if a lawmaker disagreed with a law, (i.e., immigration detention), they have the power to change it. However, these anarchists chose to attack those who enforce the law. The adage "don't shoot the messenger" seems appropriate.

Remember this: the federal government has many police agencies enforcing the law in every corner of the country. These officers and agents are law enforcement professionals trained to catch criminals who fit their specific discipline.

5. CURRENT POLICE CLIMATE

The current environment for your average police officer is dismal. In my 2016 book, *Nationwide Police Strike,* I describe the climate this way:

This is the worst time in history to be a cop. People hate you for something you didn't do nor had anything to do with. Those who don't hate you remain silent for fear of being outed or labeled a racist. Just after 9/11, people loved cops and made a special effort to thank us for doing the job. I remember just a couple of weeks after September 11, 2011, a woman grabbed me just outside a Dunkin' Donuts to thank me for being a police officer and for protecting her family. The woman was sincere and was overwhelmed with emotion as

I explained to her that it was my job and my pleasure. Police didn't do anything special to deserve that praise when two planes struck the World Trade Center. That morning, NYPD's finest officers did what they were paid to do. Cops and firefighters ran toward the danger while everyone else ran out. This is not unlike July 2016, when a rogue criminal maggot opened fire on cops protecting a Black Lives Matter protest in Dallas. When the shots rang out, protesters scurried away while the protectors in blue couldn't get there fast enough. At the time, nobody knew who the target was, only that the public was in danger. Dallas cops were doing their job. Even after this, cops continue to show up in arguably the most hostile work environment.

Those words are truer today than when written in 2016. In fact, it has become much worse. Massachusetts, for example, is going out of its way to prove to the rest of the country just how "progressive" the state is. In July 2020, as a knee-jerk reaction to calls for so-called police reform, both the senate and house have proposed bills that will undoubtedly make objective policing worse. If the house bill is passed, the way in which the average police officer deploys their use-of-force will change. Ultimately, this law will delay when the officer is allowed to go "hands-on." Allow me to explain: today, a police officer can use force to prevent a crime. For example, you're pushing a stroller down a city sidewalk and Jimmy Scumbag approaches you from behind. He loads up his fist and swings a ball of fury toward the back of your head. An astute police officer who happens to be standing along the storefront sees the impending roundhouse and leaps into action. The way the law is today, the officer is well within his lawful authority to wrap up Jimmy Scumbag before his knuckles make contact with your skull. The cop has essentially deployed a level of physical force to prevent a crime. However, if Mass bill H4860 becomes law, the officer will no longer be allowed to deploy force to stop your head from being bashed. In our scenario with Jimmy Scumbag, the officer will be required to wait until after you're punched in the back of the head before subduing Jimmy Scumbag and taking him into custody. That is the horrific way this law was written. In order for the cop to intervene before a crime is committed, he would have to prove the crime would have constituted "serious physical injury or death." A punch to the head, although painful and violent, would not fit this standard.

While reading my hypothetical scenario, you might be asking, why doesn't the cop go hands-on before Jimmy's fist meets my head, essentially violating the law? The answer is simple: liability. If the officer prematurely intervenes, the newly created Massachusetts review board will revoke his police officer license and bar him from ever being a cop again. Add to that, the criminal charges against the cop and the house he just lost when he's forced to pay damages when the town settles Jimmy Scumbag's lawsuit (which is another caveat of this law: the town is no longer responsible to pay damages). Needless to say, a cop is not putting his liberty, his home, and his children's future on the line for Jimmy Scumbag. An old, retired Boston cop summed it up perfectly: "You can get fired for doing something; you'll never get fired for doing nothing!"

What's ironic, at the precise moment when society should be making a cop's job easier, they're going out of their way to make it harder. Crime and violence are rising at an alarming rate in U.S. cities.

Add to that, where violent civil unrest and rioting are a daily occurrence, local leadership is refusing help from the federal government. The mayor of Chicago, for example, belittled the President of the United States and his outstretched hand while asking the public to stop shooting each other. If the big city leaders can't straighten out their situation and protect hard-working innocent civilians, the federal government has a duty and obligation to send their resources to fix the mess.

Enter a federal police force.

Remember this: policing must exist in order to maintain a civil society. Failure to support them is a recipe for disaster. Without order, there is chaos.

6. FEDERALIZING THE POLICE

Most advanced countries have a national police agency responsible for maintaining public order. Both our neighbors to the north and the south have federal law enforcement agencies. The Royal Canadian Mounted police (or Mounties as they're affectionately called) provide policing services to many suburban and rural provinces on a contract basis. Most of these towns have marginal crime rates which make the need of their own police department obsolete. America's counterpart to the south has the Mexican Federales as their national police agency. The Federales became the "National Guard" under the control of the Mexican Armed Forces. This agency is tasked with assisting local police with border security and civil order.

So, why is the United States uniquely without a national police force? It's written in our constitution that states are responsible for their own affairs: government, safety and the like. However, when it comes to policing, I contend this arrangement is antiquated. As I outlined in my book *Abolish the Police*, much of the law enforcement system is in need of a twentieth century overhaul.

Understand, the argument here is not to invoke martial law. In fact, it's just the opposite. Federalizing the police is about having one police standard where officers adhere to the same policy under the supervision of the federal government. For those readers who may not know, *martial law* is defined by Merriam Webster as 1: the law applied in occupied territory by the military authority of the occupying power; 2: the law administered by military forces that is invoked by a government in an emergency when the civilian law enforcement agencies are unable to maintain public order and safety.

Organization: I foresee the United States Police

Force being organized as any other national agency within the federal government. In chapter 4, we reviewed several federal law enforcement agencies that have satellite offices throughout the country. Most large cities have federal buildings that house most of these agencies. For example, the Tip O'Neill building in Boston, Massachusetts, houses the Secret Service, U.S. Marshals and the FBI. Thus, the physical infrastructure is already well established in major metropolitan areas. The only logistical hill to climb is establishing regional offices in suburban or rural areas that do not have federal facilities. This problem is easily mitigated once local police departments are defunded and dismantled. Some municipal police departments have several district police stations that can be easily converted for federal police deployment.

Each regional federal police area will be headed by a director, (or what's commonly referred to as chief of police). Under the director, the federal police will have the standard hierarchy of line and staff. This would consist of captains, lieutenants, sergeants and frontline officers. Each district will have their respective staffs that will respond to locations where the need is greatest. Services will consist of the typical calls for service any municipality receives today, including illegally parked cars and shoplifters.

Laws: The United States Police Force will enforce federal code. For example, 18 U.S. Code section 1111 is the federal code for Murder. In fact, Title 18 replaces most state criminal codes enforced by state and local law enforcement. The mere fact federal law enforcement agencies do not enforce criminal conduct on the local level does not mean they cannot. State and local officials have the responsibility to enforce state law; whereas the federal government has the responsibility to enforce federal law no matter its location.

Oftentimes federal and local law enforcement work together for a common purpose. Take, for example, bank robberies. The section for bank robbery is 1349, and because banks are insured by the federal government (i.e. FDIC), the FBI is the primary investigative agency. They look to local cops to secure the scene and conduct interviews. However, the federal government cannot force state sworn police officers to enforce federal laws.

For example, many states have legalized the possession and consumption of marijuana which is still regulated and enforced by the federal code. The DEA, for example, cannot force local city police agencies to arrest or charge those they find violating the federal code. With that being said, federal law enforcement can enforce federal laws even in states that have legalized it. The only difference between the two law enforcement disciplines is where the prisoner goes after arrest. As explained in chapter two, local cops bring their prisoners to county courts, while federal agents bring them to federal courts.

Pros: The current system of recruiting and retaining police officers in America is deeply flawed. Cops are hired by local municipalities, trained to follow local and state policy and then compensated by the community. Those policies and qualifications differ from one town to the next. They include varying levels of education and proficiency from agency to agency. As described in chapter 5, police officers represent towns, cities, states and even Native American tribes. The federal government can find the same qualified applicants as local police departments offer them better benefits packages and maintain a common ethical standard throughout the country. Appropriate policing is the same from coast to coast. What difference does it make what logo is on their paycheck?

Universal training for police officers with the universal umbrella of supervision by the federal government is the solution to the current problem with police. One agency, one government structure for police services. Only then would protestors and anti-police crybabies be able to hold all police accountable for the actions of a few. Otherwise, what happens in Minneapolis cannot reflect poorly on the police officers in Rhode Island.

What's most appealing about our new federal police system is the monetary savings and redistribution of money as they see fit. Tax payers will be relieved to save a considerable amount of money by regionalizing police services. The federal police service will have a fraction of the currently hundreds of police chiefs representing each town in the state. For example, Massachusetts has 365 municipal towns with approximately 300 police chiefs (some towns in the western part of the state use mutual aid agreements for police service). Similar to the Postal Police and Amtrak, the United States Police Force could divide Massachusetts into ten geographic districts based on population and need for police services.

Another appealing asset of the federal system is recruiting. Once local police agencies are dismantled, the best officers will be hired as federal police officers and assigned to their own neighborhoods. With the lackluster appeal of the police job having decimated recruiting for local police departments the last few years, the federal government can filter through and hire only the best candidates.

Cons: I've outlined many beneficial consequences to having a universal policing system. You may be asking, what are the drawbacks to a federal policing system? The answer in one word, is *control*. Currently, small towns with high tax brackets can afford well-staffed, high-priced police departments to react to their whims. A recent example are several towns enacting laws requiring face masks geared to slowing the spread of the coronavirus (COVID-19). The small town lawmakers then direct their police department to enforce these laws. That level of control will no longer be an option under a federal policing system.

Remember this: federal law enforcement agencies already have the tools, training and logistics to provide effective law enforcement to the American people. Dismantling, defunding and abolishing local police departments will force the federal government to step-in to provide safety and security for everybody.

7. CONCLUSION

If you demoralize, frustrate, challenge, and
personally bankrupt local police officers, eventually
they'll no longer want to police your neighborhood.
When the best applicants are no longer interested
in being a cop, less qualified cops are hired. These
replacements will not be as skilled, or mentally
prepared to do the job and a vicious cycle will
begin. These lesser qualified cops will violate the
rights of the citizens worse than in 2020. These
officers will be held accountable by a new order of
police oversight committees, mob justice and
eventually fired and imprisoned. The recruitment
cycle seeks more applicants where cities are forced
to scrape the bottom of the barrel. The town hires
less qualified applicants which cause more grief for
the public and so on. When most of them leave,
civil society will be forced to search for an

alternative public safety system.

We are at a crossroads in American policing. Officers who were hired during the community policing era of the late 80s and 90s are beginning to retire. These officers were trained like no other generation in cop history. Many of them have since moved up the chain of command in their respective police departments, training many of the early 21st century police officers. Community policing was an unbelievably successful program that drove crime rates down across the nation. The idea behind community policing programs was to embolden the street cop to forge relationships with community stakeholders and work in partnership to stop and prevent crime. Frontline cops were given tools and authority to make an impact on the street level. 2020 is the complete opposite. Cops are being discouraged to converse with the public and community members are being told the neighborhood police officer is their enemy. By introducing pro-criminal, anti-cop legislation (as described in chapter five), many states have become a breeding ground for an "us versus them" relationship. The words may not be leaving their lips, but progressive, anti-cop politicians are calling for the relentless alienation of cops, and their actions speak much louder than words. These messages are being heard loud and clear by protesters, rioters and anarchists.

As I stated in the introduction, this work is mine. The opinions expressed in the preceding pages do not represent my employer, my family, my cats or the imaginary dinosaur I had as a child. These opinions are of a sound mind and will not be suppressed.

ABOUT THE AUTHOR

Robert J. Disario has spent the majority of his adult life as a police officer in Massachusetts. He owns and operates a private security company called Suburban Security Services. Rob is a graduate of the University of Hartford (2000), and the Lowell Police Academy (2001). Rob is fortunate enough to remember a time when cops were respected and supported; however those days are a mere memory. Today, Rob's passion is his family, his writing and his security company (suburbanpatrol.com).

Rob has self-published several novellas including Cops and Robbers of Whiskey Point, Masonic Fiction: The Master's Men and Drink the Punch. Other publications include a tactical self-protection book, Protect Yourself, and an opinion editorial titled Nationwide Police Strike.

Rob is consistently inspired by his work as a police officer to write and self publish. And as any author will tell you, they don't write for the money. Writing about fictional characters is Rob's only creative outlet. He enjoys it even if he never published a word. Thanks to mediums like Amazon, Rob is able to share his creative outlet with the world.

Rob's opinions and theories are his own and do not represent any entity or other affiliation. They are based on his own experiences as an average American police officer.

www.ingramcontent.com/pod-product-compliance
Lightning Source LLC
Chambersburg PA
CBHW052322220526
45472CB00001B/223